CHRISTIAN PACIFISM AND JUST WAR THEORY
Discipleship and the Ethics of War, Violence and the Use of Force

CHRISTIAN PACIFISM AND JUST WAR THEORY

Discipleship and the Ethics of War, Violence and the Use of Force

Harold Palmer

CHRISTIAN PACIFISM AND JUST WAR THEORY
Discipleship and the Ethics of War,
Violence and the Use of Force

ISBN (13) (Paperback): 978-1-68109-031-3
ISBN (10) (Paperback): 1-68109-031-7
ISBN (13) (Kindle): 978-1-68109-032-0
ISBN (10) (Kindle): 1-68109-032-5
ISBN (13) (ePub): 978-1-68109-033-7
ISBN (10) (ePub): 1-68109-033-3

LogosLight™
an imprint of TellerBooks™
TellerBooks.com/LogosLight

www.TellerBooks.com

Manufactured in the U.S.A.

Cover: Jacques-Louis David, The Intervention of the Sabine Women
(1799, Public Domain image)

NOTE: Unless otherwise stated herein, all biblical Scriptures quoted herein are taken from the New King James Version or American Standard Version translations.

DISCLAIMER: The opinions, views, positions and conclusions expressed in this volume reflect those of the individual author and not necessarily those of the publisher or any of its imprints, editors or employees.

ABOUT THE IMPRINT

The LogosLight™ imprint first started with the collection The Church Fathers Speak, a compilation of the voices of the early Church fathers and their teachings on sanctity and Christ-like living. This ancient wisdom guides the reader on the path to cultivating holiness that yields self-dominion, patience, and virtue.

LogosLight has since grown to encompass Christian poetry and inspirational books, translations of the Bible and Hebrew Scriptures, and various Christian records and Liturgies.

LogosLight books also examine the role of Judeo-Christian thought on the formation of Western civic institutions, the moral foundations of just societies, and the role of faith in civil governance.

CONTENTS

ABBREVIATIONS

English Translations of the Bible:

ASV .... American Standard Version
BBE .... Bible in Basic English
Darby .... Darby Bible
ESV .... English Standard Version
ISV .... International Standard Version
KJV .... King James Version
MKJV .... Modern King James Version
NIV .... New International Version
NKJV .... New King James Version
RSV .... Revised Standard Version

Books of the Bible:

1Ch .... 1 Chronicles
1Co .... 1 Corinthians
1Jn .... 1 John
1Ki .... 1 Kings
1Pe .... 1 Peter
1Sa .... 1 Samuel
1Th .... 1 Thessalonians
1Ti .... 1 Timothy
2Ch .... 2 Chronicles
2Co .... 2 Corinthians
2Jn .... 2 John
2Ki .... 2 Kings
2Pe .... 2 Peter
2Sa .... 2 Samuel
2Th .... 2 Thessalonians
2Ti .... 2 Timothy
3Jo .... 3 John
Acts .... Book of Acts
Amos .... Book of Amos
Col .... Colossians
Dan .... Daniel

Deu .... Deuteronomy
Ecc .... Ecclesiastes
Eph .... Ephesians
Est .... Esther
Exo .... Exodus
Eze .... Ezekiel
Ezr .... Book of Ezra
Gal .... Galatians
Gen .... Genesis
Hab .... Habakkuk
Hag .... Haggai
Heb .... Hebrews
Hos .... Hosea
Isa .... Isaiah
Jas .... James
Jer .... Jeremiah
Job .... Book of Job
Joel .... Book of Joel
John .... Gospel of John
Jon .... Jonah
Jos .... Joshua
Jude .... Book of Jude
Jdg .... Judges
Lam .... Lamentations
Lev .... Leviticus
Luke .... Gospel of Luke
Mal .... Malachi
Mark .... Gospel of Mark
Mat .... Gospel of Matthew
Mic .... Micah
Nah .... Nahum
Neh .... Nehemiah
Num .... Numbers
Oba .... Obadiah
Phm .... Philemon
Php .... Philippians
Pro .... Proverbs
Psa .... Psalms
Rev .... Revelation
Rom .... Romans

Ruth .... Book of Ruth
Son .... Song of Solomon
Tit .... Titus
Zec .... Zechariah
Zep .... Zephaniah

CHAPTER 1. INTRODUCTION

What did Jesus mean when he said to "love your enemies" and "pray for those who persecute you" (Mat 5:38-44)? Do these commandments leave room for Christians to serve in militaries or police forces that implement the use of force? Or is the Christian to steadfastly reject violence and embrace pacifism? Are certain wars justified on the basis of just war theory, or are all wars, in their brutality and destruction, inherently evil?

In this study, we examine the case that has traditionally been made to justify Christian participation in war. We begin with a historical background of the roots of just war theory as promulgated by Thomas Aquinas. We then examine the passages on which just war theorists rely, including God's commandments to the Israelites to go to war against their enemies, Jesus' praise of the Roman Army centurion for his faith and God's use of the centurion Cornelius to graft Gentiles into the Kingdom of God. Arguing that these passages have been misunderstood, we conclude that Christianity only permits a single response to evil—self-sacrificial love.

We make the case for Christian pacifism by examining the life of Jesus and arguing that His crucifixion was more than a salvific act; it also exemplified the ideal of Christian living. Being a disciple of Jesus means emulating Him in every way, including responding to violence through self-sacrificial love, as Jesus did, and obeying Jesus' commands to be as "harmless as doves" (Mat 10:16), to "turn the other cheek" and "pray for those who persecute you" (Mat 5:38-44).

Finally, we tackle the difficult question of Old Testament violence and argue that it falls within a specific context and is not normative for members of the New Covenant of Grace. Rather than embrace violence, we are to follow the examples set by the early church and its martyrs, including the Apostle Stephen, who prayed that his persecutors not be charged with their sins (Acts 7:60), and the apostle Paul, who taught us to "live peaceably with all men" (Rom 12:18). Our war is not a physical struggle (2Co 10:3), but a spiritual war to be waged with prayer, faith and the gospel of peace (Eph 6:12-18).

CHAPTER 2. THE DEVELOPMENT OF CHRISTIAN JUST WAR THEORY

A. THE FIRST THREE CENTURIES

Christian involvement within the affairs of the State was limited during the first centuries of the Church. There were some Christians in civil service (consider the Christians within "Caesar's household" referenced by St. Paul (Php 4:22)) and in military service (both John the Baptist and Jesus ministered to soldiers (Luke 3:14; Mat 8:5-8) and the centurion Cornelius was used to bring the Gospel to the Gentiles (Act 10:35-48)). However, Christians, like other minorities in the early Roman Empire, faced persecution by the Roman government. The extent to which Christians were involved with civil government was generally limited to praying for the emperor (1Ti 2:1-2). It would have been incongruous for a Christian to join the military and support the Empire's oppression of other Christians.

The first centuries of Christianity were thus marked by pacifism with respect to military service and the use of violence. Origen (c. 184 – 253) said that Christians "do not go forth as soldiers." Tertullian (c. 160 – c. 225) wrote that only "*without* the sword can the Christian wage war: for the Lord has abolished the sword" (see Mat 26:52). Clement of Alexandria (c. 150 – c. 215) wrote that "he who holds the sword must cast it away" and "if one of the faithful becomes a soldier he must be rejected by the Church, for he has scorned God."

B. CONSTANTINE'S CONVERSION (312)

Much of this changed with Constantine's conversion to Christianity in 312 AD. After Constantine's conversion, Christianity became the official religion of the Roman Empire. Military service was no longer associated with the brutal oppression and killing of Christians on behalf of a pagan Empire. Defending the Empire from northern invasions took on new meaning and was not deemed to be inconsistent with the Gospel of peace, particularly when war was being waged in order to maintain peace or reestablish justice.

This shift in position is reflected in the writings of early Church fathers and councils. The Council of Arles (314) stated that to forbid the State "the right to go to war was to condemn it to extinction." St. Athanasius of Alexandria (293-373) wrote:

> Although one is not supposed to kill, the killing of the enemy in time of war is both a lawful and praiseworthy thing. This is why we consider individuals who have distinguished themselves in war as being worthy of great honors and indeed public monuments are set up to celebrate their achievements. It is evident, therefore, that at one particular time and under one set of circumstances, an act is not permissible, but when time and circumstances are right, it is both allowed and condoned (*The Letter of St. Athanasius to Amun*).

Shortly thereafter, Christian theologians, starting with St. Augustine, began formulating a Christian just war theory.

C. ST. AUGUSTINE (354 – 430)

For Augustine of Hippo, war was a necessary consequence of human sin and evil. God therefore instituted civil government to punish evil (Rom 13:4). Civil leaders are to use force to defend the innocent when all other forms of peaceful intervention fail. Armies are raised not to oppress and maraud, but to protect the weak and establish law, order and justice. Augustine concedes that any system of worldly justice will ultimately be marred by the effects of sin, yet conscientious Christians are to seek justice that reflects the perfect justice that we will witness in the hereafter.

Augustine observes that if Christianity "forbade war altogether, those who sought salutary advice in the Gospel would rather have been counseled to cast aside their arms and to give up soldiering altogether. On the contrary, they were told: 'Do violence to no man ... and be content with your pay.' If he commanded them to be content with their pay, he did not forbid soldiering" (Thomas Aquinas, *Summa Theologica*, II-II, q. 40 a.1 (quoting Augustine)).

It would seem that Augustine's justification of the legitimacy of war is contrary to Jesus' teaching to not "resist evil" and to "turn the other cheek" (Mat 5:39). Yet Augustine argues that Jesus teaches the law of grace that governs the kingdom of God, which is "within you" (Luke 17:21). While the law of grace is to govern man's interior spiritual life of the kingdom of God, Christians are also subject to another, worldly kingdom, which is governed by the law of justice "for your own good" (Rom 13:4).

While the Christian is to love and forgive his enemy on the spiritual level, according to the law of grace, he is nonetheless to seek justice (Mic 6:8. For example, if a Christian is assaulted and robbed, he is to first forgive his "enemy." But he is not to eschew justice; rather he is to actively seek it. This may take on many forms, such as seeing to the criminal's arrest and punishment by the civil authorities, thus furthering the State's divinely-appointed purpose of punishing evil (Rom 13:4). This is not inconsistent with loving his "enemy" or visiting or ministering to him while he is in prison.

One thus sees in Augustine's work a dichotomy between the kingdom of God and the kingdoms of the world. He argues that Christ's injunction to "turn the other cheek" applies only to the interior life. A just war is according to Augustine one that seeks to punish evildoers, in the spirit of Romans 13:4 and reestablish peace, order and the rule of law. War can then be said for Augustine to be an instrument of peace.

D. ST. THOMAS AQUINAS (1225 – 1274)

St. Thomas Aquinas built upon the just war foundation developed by Augustine and introduced the concept of the common good as a necessary element in the legality of war. To be legitimate, a military must have as its goal the defense of the public good, which includes the right to worship God. Soldiers are therefore instruments of the civil authority instituted by God, which guarantee civil order and stability.

Aquinas then lays down his conditions for just war, which must be waged: (i) by a legitimate authority; (ii) with a just cause; and (iii) a right intention. This theory over the centuries came to incorporate other elements, including the exhaustion of all non-violent options and a reasonable prospect of success, further elaborated below.

CHAPTER 3. MODERN CHURCH VIEWS

A. THE CATHOLIC CHURCH

The Benedictine Monks of Solesmes, France, provide a succinct overview of the Catholic Church's teaching on the use of force in *Just War at the Service of the Divine Precept of Peace*, which observes that:

> [P]eace can have recourse to force. However, force, in itself, is incapable of restoring peace, since peace is the fruit of the union of justice and charity. Some enemies of justice cannot be led to accept the necessary conditions for peace without the use of force. The importance of a certain good justifies entirely its defense by force against an unjust aggression (Moines de Solesmes, *La Paix Internationale*, Desclee, Paris, 1956, v. I, p. 20).

The *Catechism of the Catholic Church* has expanded Aquinas' three just war conditions (legitimate authority, just cause and right intention) and expanded his list with four additional conditions. Today, the Catholic Church requires a war to meet the following criteria in order for it to classify as "just":

1. Legitimate Authority

It must be waged by a legitimate civil authority (*i.e.*, a State, in accordance with Romans 13), not individuals or groups who do not constitute an authority sanctioned by whatever the society deems legitimate;

2. Just Cause

The cause must be just (*i.e.*, self-defense of the innocent against an armed attack, redressing an injury, punishing evil, restoring territory unjustly seized);

3. Right Intention

The central intention of the war must be reestablishing a just peace (not conquering, spreading seeds of revolt or acquiring power or material possessions);

4. Last Resort

All non-violent options must be exhausted before the use of force is justified;

5. Reasonable Prospect of Success

Deaths and injury incurred in a war not having a reasonable chance of success are not morally justifiable;

6. Grave Damage from the Aggressor

The damage inflicted by the aggressor on the nation must be lasting, grave and certain;

7. Proportionality

The use of arms must not produce evils graver than the evil to be eliminated; the peace established by the war must be preferable to the peace that would have prevailed had the war not been fought.

B. OTHER CHURCHES

While Catholic just war theory is perhaps the most developed and precise statement of the justification of war among the various Christian denominations, it is not universally accepted by Christian churches, many of which have their own traditions or reject just war theory altogether, believing war to be incompatible with Jesus' command to not "resist an evildoer" (Mat 5:39) and St. Paul's teaching to never "repay anyone evil for evil" (Rom 12:17).

While some Christians reject the use of force under any circumstances, the World Council of Churches' "Ecumenical Call to Just Peace" (2011) perhaps best captures the views of most Protestant and Orthodox Christians. The statement calls for nonviolent resistance, the transformation of conflict and just peace towards "God's purpose for humanity and all creation" (Cl. 12), but recognizes that there are "extreme circumstances where, as the last resort and the lesser evil, the lawful use of armed force may become necessary" (Cl. 22).

1. The Eastern Orthodox Church

There is no ethical teaching for just war in the writings of the Greek Orthodox Church fathers. War, even in unavoidable circumstances, is deemed an "evil," albeit a lesser of evils in certain circumstances. According to Fr. Stanley Harakas, the Greek Fathers never elaborate a just war theory and instead take a pro-peace stance on the question of war.

St. John Chrysostom (347 – 407), bishop of Constantinople, for example, distinguishes between Christians, who are "not permitted forcibly to correct the failings of those who sin" and the civil authority, who "when they have captured malefactors under the law, show their authority to be great and prevent them even against their will from following their own devices." In the case of Christians, "the wrong-doer must be made better, not by force, but by persuasion (St. John Chrysostom, "On the Priesthood").

Emperor Nicephoros Phocas of Byzantium (963 – 969) requested the Orthodox Church to recognize soldiers dying at war to be classified as "martyrs." The Church denied the request on the basis that under St. Basil's Canon 13, those who kill others in war are prevented from Communion for three years. They should not therefore be deemed equal to the holy martyrs.

The Ecumenical Patriarch of the Orthodox Christian Church Bartholomew I, in his October 22, 1999 address in Novi Sad, Serbia, said:

> War and violence are never means used by God in order to achieve a result. They are for the most part machinations of the devil used to achieve unlawful ends. ... [I]n a few specific cases, the Orthodox Church forgives an armed defense against oppression and violence. However, as a rule, peaceful resolution of differences and peaceful cooperation are more pleasing to God and more beneficial to humankind. War and violence breed hatred and revenge, leading to an endless cycle of evil until opponents completely annihilate each other. For this reason St. Paul exhorts us, "Do not be overcome by evil, but overcome evil with good" (Rom 12:21).

In this light, Fr. Paul O'Callaghan, a priest of the Antiochian Orthodox Church, points to the repeated invocation of "peace" in the Orthodox Christian liturgy of St. John Chrysostom, which begins with "in peace, let us pray to the Lord" and continues with "for the peace from above and the salvation of our souls. He writes that "every form of conflict and strife is a manifestation of sin" and that warfare "belongs to realm of fallen human existence and can in no way embody the justice, righteousness and indeed peace that are the very essence of the reconciliation of God and humanity."

At the same time, however, the liturgy includes petitions for the armed forces: "we pray for this country, ... civil authorities and armed forces"; "Grant peace to ... the armed forces." Nonetheless, the taking of human life is "always considered an objective evil, even when done in the pursuit of a 'just cause'" (Fr. Paul O'Callaghan, "Peace and War in The Eastern Orthodox Church," *Messenger*, December 2002).

This seeming paradox can be reconciled by recognizing the application of *economia*, or dispensation in light of human weakness, to the strict principles of *akrievia* embodied in canon law. Like divorce, war is allowed not because it is good, but because of the frailty of fallen nature. Yet like marital integrity, peace is the norm and goal of Christian life and war is deemed sin. Regardless of its cause or intention, war is never characterized as "just" in the Eastern tradition, which has consequently never elaborated a just war theory (Fr. Paul O'Callaghan, "Peace and War in The Eastern Orthodox Church," *Messenger*, December 2002).

2. The Anglican Church

Individual Anglicans hold different views with respect to just war. Some accept Augustine's just war theory; others adhere to a strictly pacifist position. The Anglican Church as a body has never articulated a just war theory.

3. The Pacifist / Anabaptist Tradition: Mennonites and the Quakers

The Mennonites and the Quakers (The Religious Society of Friends) are denominations that arose out of the Protestant Reformation that embrace pacifism. Mennonites believe Christ's teachings to "love your enemies" and "do good to those who hate you" (Mat 5:44) prevent them from participating in military campaigns against other countries.

The Quakers are totally committed to non-violence. In 1660, the Quakers declared "...the spirit of Christ which leads us into all Truth will never move us to fight and war against any man with outward weapons, neither for the kingdom of Christ, nor for the kingdoms of the world."

4. Within Catholicism: Fr. Emmanuel McCarthy

Fr. Emmanuel Charles McCarthy, a priest of the Eastern Rite (Byzantine-Melkite) of the Catholic Church, is a prominent spokesperson of Christian pacifism. He argues that the purpose of the Church, the salvation of souls, can never be subordinated to any other purpose, including the survival of an individual or State, whether through violence or other means. He concedes that the Catholic Church has developed a just war theory, but argues that St. Augustine, the father of the theory, never acknowledged that any war could meet the standards of a just war, thus rendering the idea no more than an elusive theory. Moreover, while a Christian has the right to follow Jesus' teaching in order to ensure her spiritual, eternal life, she does *not* have a right to depart from Jesus' teaching of non-violence in order to preserve her physical, temporal life.

5. Within the Evangelical Church: Pastor Greg Boyd

American theologian and pastor Greg Boyd sharply criticizes Augustine's dichotomy between the life of the spirit, which requires love and forgiveness and the life of the flesh, which allows for war to punish evil on the basis of justice. He argues that Augustine's approach "makes complete nonsense of Jesus' teaching" (*The Myth of a Christian Nation*, Zondervan, p. 163). "In this way, Jesus' radical teachings get divorced from actual behavior, a concept that has plagued Christianity to this day. No one exposes the harm to this impossible divorce has wrought in Christendom as well as Camp does in *Mere Discipleship*" (*id.*, p. 205).

CHAPTER 4. DO THE SCRIPTURES TEACH PACIFISM OR JUST WAR?

A. THE JUST WAR POSITION

1. Old Testament

a. Go "to War against Your Enemies" (Deu 20:1)

Deuteronomy 20:1, which discusses the context of going "to war against your enemies," sets the general tone for Israel's relations with her enemies. It was one of war and destruction rather than self-sacrificial submission and love.

b. Destruction of Israel's Enemies throughout the Old Testament

The destruction of Heshbon, Bashan, Amalek and many other nations throughout the Hebrew Scriptures serve as concrete examples of this vengeance against Israel's enemies.

Many of these examples can be read as examples of God's using Israel as an agent to carry out punishment for these nations' sins, but Jericho is also utterly destroyed by the Israelites, and the only fault I can extrapolate from the Scriptures is the fact that they inhabited in the land that God promised to the Israelites.

The relations between Israel and their arch-enemies, the Philistines, is marked by violence rather than by self-sacrificial love. Consider, for example, when God sends His Spirit upon Samson to bring death and destruction against the Philistines.

c. Advice on Waging War (Deuteronomy, Proverbs, etc.)
   - "Hear, O Israel: Today you are on the verge of battle with your enemies. Do not let your heart faint, do not be afraid, and do not tremble or be terrified because of them" (Deu 20:3).
   - "So don't go to war without wise guidance; victory depends on having many advisers" (Pro 24:6) (NIV).

d. We Should Not Seek the Prosperity or Peace of the Ammonites or Moabites (Deu 23)
   - Deu 23:3 "An Ammonite or Moabite shall not enter the assembly of the Lord; even to the tenth generation none of his descendants shall enter the assembly of the Lord forever,
   - Deu 23:4 because they did not meet you with bread and water on the road when you came out of Egypt, and because they hired against you Balaam the son of Beor from Pethor of Mesopotamia, to curse you.
   - Deu 23:5 Nevertheless the Lord your God would not listen to Balaam, but the Lord your God turned the curse into a blessing for you, because the Lord your God loves you.
   - Deu 23:6 You shall not seek their peace nor their prosperity all your days forever.

2. New Testament

a. Jesus and Peter's Sword

a. *Overview: Peter Is Not Rebuked for Carrying a Sword*

Pacifists point to the account at Gethsemane, where Jesus rebuked Peter for applying force to defend Him, as evidence of Jesus' pacifist position. However, this account fails to provide an adequate explanation as to why Peter carried a sword to begin with. Sword are weapons of violence; had Jesus completely eschewed violence, why did he even permit his disciple to carry one?

b. Pacifist Response: It is an Argument Drawn from Silence

The pacifist response to this critique is that it is an argument drawn from silence. Just because the Scriptures do not contain an account in which Peter (or other disciples) are rebuked for carrying a sword does not mean that they were never rebuked.

c. Problem with the Pacifist Response: Jesus Tells Peter to Put His Sword in its Place, Not to Discard His Sword

After Jesus rebukes Peter for cutting off the servant's ear, He does not tell him to discard his sword. Rather, He tells him to "Put your sword in its place" (Mat 26:52). Had the sword *always* been off limits for Christians, it is unlikely that Peter would have been carrying the sword to begin with and, if he were carrying it, it is likely that Jesus would have told Peter to discard it rather than put it back "in its place" after Peter had used it. Jesus' command indicates that there is a time and place for violence, but the arrest scene at Gethsemane was not one of them.

d. Pacifist Response: Peter was Not Carrying a Sword, But Rather a Knife for Survival in the Wilderness

Strong assigns G3162 to μάχαιρα (*machaira*, pronounced mä'-khī-rä), which is used in the original Greek. The Blue Letter Bible defines the term as follows:

> I. a large knife, used for killing animals and cutting up flesh
> II. a small sword, as distinguished from a large sword
> A. curved sword, for a cutting stroke
> B. a straight sword, for thrusting.

Pacifists adopt definition I and argue that Peter was merely carrying around a knife, a tool that was necessary to survive in the wilderness. Thus, when Jesus told Peter to put the *machaira* in its place (Mat 26:52), He was not in any way endorsing the possession of a deadly weapon to be used against humans.

e. *Problem with the Pacifist Response: Every Major Bible Translation Defines Machaira as "Sword"*

Every Bible translation that I have consulted (ASV, BBE, Darby, ESV, FDB, FLS, ISV, KJV, LBLA, MKJV, NKJV, RSV, SRV, SSE, SVD) translates the term as "sword" (in the case of French, "épée"; Spanish, "espada"; Arabic, سيف), which supports the just war theory, since Jesus told Peter to put his sword back into its place (Mat 26:52). There is a remote possibility that all of these translations got it wrong and Peter was merely carrying around a large knife for survival in the wilderness, but it is highly unlikely.

f. *Pacifist Reply: The Major Bible Translations Are Colored by the Doctrinal Presuppositions of the Translators*

Pacifists reply that the Greek *machaira*, which should properly be translated as a "knife," is erroneously translated as "sword" in translations colored by the erroneous doctrinal presuppositions of the translators, including, for example, the Christ would allow his disciples to carry around lethal weapons and that He would command Peter to put such a weapon "in its place" (Mat 26:52), rather than discard it.

g. *Problem with the Pacifist Reply: Other Instances of the Greek* Machaira *Imply the Use of a Sword*

Throughout the New Testament, the Greek *machaira* (μάχαιρα - G3162) is used within a context that would more accurately translate as a sword, a weapon of violent force, than as a knife or tool for survival.

The following are all of the verses in the New Testament in which the Greek *machaira* appears (KJV). In the first group, the Greek *machaira* clearly falls within a context of violence, thus unambiguously translating as "sword." In the second group, the Greek *machaira* could potentially be translated as "knife."

Instances in which the translation of "sword" is unequivocal because of the surrounding verses, which imply the use of *machaira* as an instrument of violent force:

- Mat 10:34 Think not that I am come to send peace on earth: I came not to send peace, but a *sword*.
- Mat 26:47 And while he yet spake, lo, Judas, one of the twelve, came, and with him a great multitude with *swords* and staves, from the chief priests and elders of the people.
- Mat 26:55 In that same hour said Jesus to the multitudes, Are ye come out as against a thief with *swords* and staves for to take me? I sat daily with you teaching in the temple, and ye laid no hold on me.
- Mar 14:43 And immediately, while he yet spake, cometh Judas, one of the twelve, and with him a great multitude with *swords* and staves, from the chief priests and the scribes and the elders.
- Luk 21:24 And they shall fall by the edge of the *sword*, and shall be led away captive into all nations: and Jerusalem shall be trodden down of the until the times of the be fulfilled.
- Luk 22:49 When they which were about him saw what would follow, they said unto him, Lord, shall we smite with the *sword*?
- Act 12:1 Now about that time Herod the king stretched out his hand to harass some from the church. Act 12:2 And he killed James the brother of John with the *sword*.
- Act 16:27 And the keeper of the prison awaking out of his sleep, and seeing the prison doors open, he drew out his

sword, and would have killed himself, supposing that the prisoners had been fled.

- Rom 8:35 Who shall separate us from the love of Christ? shall tribulation, or distress, or persecution, or famine, or nakedness, or peril, or *sword*?

- Rom 13:4 For he is the minister of to thee for good. But if thou do that which is evil, be afraid; for he beareth not the *sword* in vain: for he is the minister of a revenger to execute wrath upon him that doeth evil.

- Eph 6:17 And take the helmet of salvation, and the *sword* of the Spirit, which is the word of God.[1]

- Heb 11:34 Quenched the violence of fire, escaped the edge of the *sword*, out of weakness were made strong, waxed valiant in fight, turned to flight the armies of the aliens.

- Heb 11:37 They were stoned, they were sawn asunder, were tempted, were slain with the *sword*: they wandered about in sheepskins and goatskins; being destitute, afflicted, tormented;

- Rev 13:10 He that leadeth into captivity shall go into captivity: he that killeth with the *sword* must be killed with the *sword*.

- Rev 13:14 And deceiveth them that dwell on the earth by the means of those miracles which he had power to do in the sight of the beast; saying to them that dwell on the earth, that they should make an image to the beast, which had the wound by a *sword*, and did live.

Instances in which *machaira* could potentially be translated as "knife":

- Mat 26:51 And, behold, one of them which were with Jesus stretched out his hand, and drew his *sword*, and struck a servant of the high priest's, and smote off his ear.

---

[1] That *machaira* here properly translates as "sword" is made clear by the surrounding verses, which include other war symbols, such as shields and helmets.

- Mat 26:52 Then said Jesus unto him, Put up again thy *sword* into his place: for all they that take the *sword* shall perish with the *sword*.
- Mar 14:47 And one of them that stood by drew a *sword*, and smote a servant of the high priest, and cut off his ear.
- Mar 14:48 And Jesus answered and said unto them, Are ye come out, as against a thief, with *swords* and with staves to take me?
- Luk 22:36 Then said he unto them, But now, he that hath a purse, let him take it, and likewise his scrip: and he that hath no *sword*, let him sell his garment, and buy one.
- Luk 22:38 And they said, Lord, behold, here are two *swords*. And he said unto them, It is enough.
- Luk 22:52 Then Jesus said unto the chief priests, and captains of the temple, and the elders, which were come to him, Be ye come out, as against a thief, with *swords* and staves?
- Joh 18:10 Then Simon Peter having a *sword* drew it, and smote the high priest's servant, and cut off his right ear. The servant's name was Malchus.
- Joh 18:11 Then said Jesus unto Peter, Put up thy *sword* into the sheath: the cup which my Father hath given me, shall I not drink it?
- Heb 4:12 For the word of is quick, and powerful, and sharper than any two-edged *sword*, piercing even to the dividing asunder of soul and spirit, and of the joints and marrow, and is a discerner of the thoughts and intents of the heart.
- Rev 6:4 And there went out another horse that was red: and power was given to him that sat thereon to take peace from the earth, and that they should kill one another: and there was given unto him a great *sword*.

b. Encounters with Roman Soldiers

a. *John the Baptist, Jesus and Peter Never Command the Romans Soldiers that They Encounter to Abandon the Military*

The New Testament contains various accounts in which John the Baptist, Jesus and Peter encounter Roman soldiers. Had military service been incompatible with being a member of Kingdom of God, surely John the Baptist, Jesus and Peter would have made some note of this or they would have counseled the soldiers to abandon the military. Rather, we read the following:

- John the Baptist merely forbids the solders from violently oppressing anyone (Luke 3:14);
- Jesus praises a Roman centurion for his faith (Mat 8);
- God uses a Roman centurion to teach Peter that the new covenant is intended for the Gentiles as well as for the Jews (Acts 10); and
- The book of Acts references a "devout soldier" (Acts 10).

b. *Commentary on Relevant Passages*

i. John the Baptist Did Not Counsel Roman Soldiers to Give Up Their Arms (Luke 3:14)

John the Baptist was a forerunner of Jesus, preaching that "kingdom of heaven is at hand" (Mat 3:2). His message was a prophecy of the kingdom of heaven to come. When soldiers came to him and asked him what they must do, he replied, "Do not intimidate anyone or accuse falsely and be content with your wages" (Luke 3:14). Never did he say that they should depart from the military. The fact that he said they should be content with their wages implies that they should accept their wages and that the institution of military service is not incompatible with the Kingdom of Heaven.

As St. Augustine observed, if Christianity "forbade war altogether, those who sought salutary advice in the Gospel would rather have been counseled to cast aside their arms, and to give up soldiering altogether. On the contrary, they were told: 'Do violence to no man ... and be content with your pay'" (Thomas Aquinas, *Summa Theologica*, II-II, q. 40 a.1 (quoting Augustine)). If John the Baptist commanded soldiers to not intimidate or accuse anyone falsely and be content with their pay (Luke 3:14), then he was at least implicitly giving legitimacy to militaries.

ii. Jesus Praised the Centurion for His Faith (Mat 8)

When Jesus entered Capernaum, a centurion pleaded with Jesus to heal his servant. He said that he was not worthy of Jesus' coming under his roof, but only asked that Jesus "speak a word, and my servant will be healed" (Mat 8:5-8). Jesus marveled at his faith, and declared that he had "not found such great faith, not even in Israel" (Mat 8:10). After he praised the centurion, He did not command him to give up his arms or resign from the military or that the military life was one of sin. Rather, he tells him, "Go your way; and as you have believed, so let it be done for you" (Mat 8:13).

While Jesus does not point out to the centurion that his military service was sin, Jesus does not hesitate to point out sin in other instances where such sin needed to be corrected:

- Jesus condemned the scribes and Pharisees as "hypocrites" who are like "whitewashed tombs which indeed appear beautiful outwardly, but inside are full of dead men's bones and all uncleanness" (Mat 23:27);
- He drove out those who bought and sold at the temple and "overturned the tables of the money changers and the seats of those who sold doves" (Mat 21:12), making "a whip of cords" and driving them "all out of the temple, with the sheep and the oxen" (John 2:15);
- Jesus said to the woman caught in the act of adultery (John 8:1-4) to "go and sin no more" (John 8:11);
- When the Samarian asked Jesus to give him the water so that she would no longer thirst (John 4:15), Jesus asked her to call her husband (John 4:16). Indeed, Jesus was pointing out an area in the woman's life that was not right with God:

she had five husbands and the one she was with at that time was not her husband (John 4:18).

iii. God Used the Centurion Cornelius to Graft Gentiles into the Kingdom of God (Acts 10)

We can look to the centurion Cornelius as another example of a soldier who was praised by God. He is highly regarded as a "devout man and one who feared God with all his household, who gave alms generously to the people, and prayed to God always" (Acts 10:2), so much so that an angel of God came to him and declared that his prayers and alms "have come up for a memorial before God" (Acts 10:3-4). Cornelius is not only described as "a just man, one who fears God and has a good reputation among all the nation of the Jews," but also as one who was "divinely instructed by a holy angel" (Acts 10:22), and who was used to bring the Gospel of Christ to the Gentiles (Acts 10:35-48). The fact that of all of the Gentiles, God used a soldier to graft Gentiles into the Kingdom of God gives an imprimatur to the institution of the military.

iv. A Second "Devout Soldier" (Acts 10)

The compatibility of godliness with military service is further confirmed by another reference in the book of Acts to a "devout soldier" whom Cornelius calls on (Acts 10:7). As this example makes clear, it is possible to be both in the military and a follower of God.

c. The Garden at Gethsemane and Calvary: Jesus' Nonviolence is not Normative for Christians

Just war theorists hold that Jesus' nonviolence at Gethsemane and on Calvary is not normative for Christians; rather, this non-violence was necessary in order to fulfill the Scriptures and God's plan to satisfy His wrath and bring forgiveness for the sins of man through a final sacrifice—that of God's only son, Jesus Christ. Had Jesus exercised violence in the defense of justice, in the pattern established in the Old Testament, God's plan never would have been complete, and man would have been left without redemption. That Jesus surrendered without violence was to fulfill the Old Testament prophecy that Jesus was to be "brought as a lamb to the slaughter, and as a sheep before her shearers is dumb, so he openeth not his mouth" (Isa 53:7). Jesus acknowledges this fact when advising his disciples against drawing their swords and defending his life through violence; He says: "How then could the Scriptures be fulfilled, that it must happen thus?" (Mat 26:54).

B. THE PACIFIST POSITION

1. Old Testament

a. Overview: Old Testament Principles, But not Specific Law or Commands, Are Applicable to Christians

Old Testament laws specifically given to the Israelites and commands given to specific generations of the Israelites are inapplicable to Christians because Old Testament theocracy is discontinuous. The Council of Jerusalem thus specifically held that the Mosaic law does not pertain to Christians (Acts 15). Moreover, God issued specific orders to Israel to destroy her enemies as punishment for sin. Such direct commands given to prophets such as Moses ordering the extinction of certain peoples cannot be said to be in continuous application today.

At the same time, however, principles that pervade the Old Testament text, such as forgiveness and love of enemies, continue to apply to Christians because they are reflections of God's unchanging character rather than commands given in the form of a law that has since been fulfilled.

b. Old Testament Principles Applicable to Christians Teach Love of Enemies

a. *The Old Testament Does Not Teach "Hatred of Enemies": Fr. Cornelius a Lapide*

Jesus says, You have heard it said, "You shall love your neighbor and hate your enemy" (Mat 5:43). However, "hate your enemy" was never commanded by any of the prophets.

Fr. Cornelius a Lapide (1567 – 1637), a Flemish Jesuit and exegete, explains this by writing that

> this saying was not in the Law, but was said by the Scribes who interpreted the Law. For they, because they found in Lev. xix. 18, 'Thou shalt love thy neighbour,' or 'thy friend,' as the Vulgate translates, inferred from thence that they should hate their enemies. Wherefore Christ here corrects this interpretation of theirs, and explains the Law, that by neighbor or friend every man is meant, even a foreigner, a Gentile, and an enemy. For all men are neighbors, through their first forefather, Adam, and brethren one of another. We are also brethren through our second Father, Christ, through whom we have been born again, and, as it were, created anew in the likeness of God, and called to the common inheritance of God, our Father in heaven.

Hence, Christ abolishes the false teachings and legal misinterpretations of the Scribes and restores the original meaning of the Scriptures.

b. *What the Old Testament Teaches about Loving One's Enemies*

i. One Should Help His Enemy

"If you meet your enemy's ox or his donkey going astray, you shall surely bring it back to him again. If you see the donkey of one who hates you lying under its burden, and you would refrain from helping it, you shall surely help him with it" (Exo 23:4-5).

ii. One Should Give His Enemy Food and Drink (Pro 25:21-22)

"If your enemy is hungry, give him bread to eat; And if he is thirsty, give him water to drink; For so you will heap coals of fire on his head, And the LORD will reward you" (Pro 25:21-22).

iii. One Should Not Rejoice When His Enemy Falls (Pro 24:17-18)

"Do not rejoice when your enemy falls, And do not let your heart be glad when he stumbles; Lest the LORD see it, and it displease Him" (Pro 24:17-18).

c. Old Testament Extermination Narratives Are Inapplicable to Christians

a. Theocracy is Discontinuous

Theocracy, as described by the Old Testament narratives, is discontinuous. One cannot read the historical narratives in which Israel was commanded to wipe out cities or peoples apart from an overriding theological awareness that Israel was a theocratic society, and therefore, not to be duplicated or used as a (future) blueprint.

b. Even if Theocracy Were Continuous, the Commands to Wipe Out Peoples Were Not Laws

Yet even if theocracy were continuous and the laws given to the Israelites could be said to be applicable to Christians today, the commands to wipe out peoples were not laws but rather specific injunctions. God did not issue a "law" to wipe out the Midianites (Num 25) as he gave, for example, a law to keep the Sabbath (Exo 20:8). The former was a command for a particular generation in a particular place at a particular time; the latter was intended as a universal law to govern all of the Israelites.

c. Only God Can Make Decisions on Life and Death; He Issued Specific Orders to Israel to Destroy Her Enemies as Punishment for Sin; These Commands Do Not Extend Beyond Israel

The Bible never grants Christians (or Jews) a general injunction to make war on or destroy the wicked. Rather, we see throughout the Bible that death is the natural consequence of sin, and God uses the Israelites in specific instances and with specific commandments to carry out this consequence. Consider, for example:

- Destruction of the people of Heshbon as punishment for blocking the people of God from realizing God's Will (Deu 2);
- Destruction of Bashan (Deu 3) and Amalek (1Sa 15) as punishment for attacking the Israelites;
- Commanding the Israelites to attack, harass, and ultimately destroy the Midianites as a punishment for harassing and seducing the Israelites (Num 25);
- Destruction of the seven nations to prevent the Israelites from engaging in the idolatry of their foes (Deu 7);
- Destruction of Jericho because of the sinful abominations of the Canaanites (Jos 6).

In each of these cases, God uses the Israelites as instruments of punishment, in the same way that He used fire and brimstone to destroy Sodom and Gomorrah for their "very grave" sins (Gen 18:20).

Nothing in the above passages gives a general sanction for violence. Rather, each case indicates a specific instance in which God commanded the Israelites to destroy their enemies. The commandments were related to specific peoples in specific points in time (*e.g.i*, to destroy the Midianites) and were never general (*e.g.*, destroy all peoples who seduce you). Moreover, the instructions were always directed at the Israelites and never to the larger covenant of believers who would be grafted into the Kingdom of God in the New Testament. One thus cannot read God's specific instructions given to the Israelites to destroy the inhabitants of Canaan as general commands available to all Christians to take up arms against their enemies.

d. The Council of Jerusalem Held that the Mosaic Law Does not Pertain to Christians (Acts 15)

Yet even if one were to read God's specific commands to the Israelites to destroy the inhabitants of Canaan as general instructions or laws pertaining to violence, the Apostles in the Council of Jerusalem held that all such laws, with the exception of prohibitions against things offered to false gods, blood, things put to death in ways which are against the law and the evil desires of the body (Acts 15:29), were inapplicable to Christians. Consider:

> Certain men taught that without circumcision, after the rule of Moses, there is no salvation (Acts 15:1). After Paul and Barnabas had arguments and discussion with them, the brothers made a decision to send Paul and Barnabas and certain others of them to the Apostles and the rulers of the church at Jerusalem about this question (Acts 15:2). When they came to Jerusalem, some of the Pharisees, who were of the faith, got up and said, It is necessary for these to have circumcision and to keep the law of Moses (Acts 15:4-5). The Apostles and the rulers of the church convened and gave thought to the question (Acts 15:6). After much discussion, Peter got up and said to them, My brothers, you have knowledge that some time back it was God's pleasure that by my mouth the good news might be given to the Gentiles so that they might have faith (Acts 15:7). And God, giving them the Holy Spirit even as he did to us (Acts 15:8), making no division between them and us, but making clean their hearts by faith (Acts 15:9). Why then are you testing God, by putting on their necks a yoke so hard that not even our fathers or we were strong enough for it? (Acts 15:10). But we have faith that we will get salvation through the grace of the Lord Jesus in the same way as they (Acts 15:11). Barnabas and Paul gave an

account of the signs and wonders which God had done among the Gentiles by them (Acts 15:12). James then said (Acts 15:13) that his decision was to not put trouble in the way of those who from among the Gentiles are turned to God (Acts 15:19) but that they only be ordered to keep themselves from things offered to false gods, from the evil desires of the body, from the flesh of animals put to death in ways against the law and from blood (Acts 15:20).

e. *The Commands Given to Israel were to Govern a Nation; Christ's Commands Govern the Individual*

The commands given to Israel were to govern a nation, whereas the commands given by Christ were to govern the individual. In order for Israel to exist as a nation, there had to be a form of justice, but Christ calls the Christian a different kingdom governed by love, mercy and forgiveness.

2. New Testament

a. Verses that Seem to Endorse Violence; Refutation

a. *Jesus Commands Purchasing a Sword (Luke 22:36); Two Swords "Is Enough" (Luke 22:38)*

i. Text

Jesus said: "he who has a money bag, let him take it, and likewise a knapsack; and he who has no sword, let him sell his garment and buy one. For I say to you that this which is written must still be accomplished in Me: 'and He was numbered with the transgressors.' For the things concerning Me have an end" (Luke 22:36-37).

Jesus' disciples said, "Lord, look, here are two swords." And He said to them, "It is enough" (Luke 22:38).

ii. Analysis

(1) Jesus Meant, "It Is Enough"

At first glance, these verses appear to endorse violence (*i.e.*, self-defense through the use of the sword). Jesus' reply, "It is enough," to his disciples seems to further bolster the view that Jesus is endorsing violence. However, the leading biblical commentaries, including Wesley's, interpret Jesus' words as meaning not that two swords were enough for the disciples to defend themselves, but rather, as a reprimand to the disciples who obstinately interpreted his statement about swords literally. He was saying, "that's enough—you obviously did not catch my point," which was not that the disciples should prepare to fight for their lives in Jesus' defense, but rather, that there were tough times ahead; Jesus would soon leave the disciples and they would be forced to fend for themselves.

In his commentary, Barnes remarks that Jesus "did not say 'the two swords are enough,' but 'it is enough;' perhaps meaning simply, enough has been said. Other matters press on, and you will yet understand what I mean.

Clark's commentary states that Jesus' words "cannot be well understood as being an answer to the supposed command of Christ, for every one who had no sword to go and sell his garment and buy one; for, in this case, they were not enough, or sufficient, as nine of the disciples must be without any instrument of defense; but they may be understood as pointing out the readiness and determination of Peter, and perhaps some others, to defend our Lord." While Clarke concedes that he does not understand the matter of the swords, he suspects that the meaning is that "there is enough said on the subject."

(2) Even If Jesus Were Literally Commanding the Purchase of
    Swords, He Did Not Intend for the Swords to be Used in
    Violence

Yet even if Jesus did literally mean that the disciples should purchase swords, the scene recounted at Garden of Gethsemane demonstrates that Jesus did not intend for the swords to be used violently against men. Just a few verses after Jesus' controversial words at Luke 22:38, He refused to defend himself against his mob of accusers and healed the servant whose ear was cut off by Peter (Luke 22:51) (see discussion under "Permit Even This," below).

b. *After Peter Slays the High Priest's Servant's Ear, Jesus Says, "Permit Even This" (Luke 22:51)*

i.   Text

> Luke 22:49   When those around Him saw what was going to happen, they said to Him, "Lord, shall we strike with the sword?"
> Luke 22:50   And one of them struck the servant of the high priest and cut off his right ear.
> Luke 22:51   But Jesus answered and said, "Permit even this." And He touched his ear and healed him.

Jesus' words "Permit even this" (Luke 22:51) can be interpreted as a ratification of Peter's brash act of striking off the high priest's servant's ear.

ii. Context

However, the context of the passage and Jesus' own actions negate such an interpretation:

-   Rather than endorse Peter's violent act, He scolded Peter, saying, "Put your sword in its place, for all who take the sword will perish by the sword" (Mat 26:52).
-   Had Jesus endorsed Peter's violence, He would have applied violence in His own defense. Jesus had the power to defend Himself and said to His disciples, "do you think that I cannot now pray to My Father, and He will provide Me with more than twelve legions of angels?" (Mat 26:53). Instead, Jesus repudiated the use of violence and willingly submitted to His accusers.

- Rather than escalate the violence against His accusers, Jesus "touched [the servant's] ear and healed him" (Luke 22:51).

Based on this context, the chief commentaries on the Scriptures have understood Jesus' words "Permit even this" (Luke 22:51) not as a ratification of Peter's violence (*i.e.*, as permitting the disciples to do violence), but rather, as a request to His accusers to allow him to heal the servant's ear. Wesley, for example, interprets Luke 22:51 as meaning, "Suffer me at least to have my hands at liberty thus far, while I do one more act of mercy." This is the interpretation that can be reconciled with the context of Luke 22 and Jesus' willing surrender at Gethsemane.

c. Encounters with Roman Soldiers

i. Overview

As discussed earlier, the New Testament contains various accounts in which John the Baptist, Jesus and Peter encounter Roman soldiers. Just war theorists argue that had military service been incompatible with being a member of Kingdom of God, surely John the Baptist, Jesus and Peter would have made some note of this or they would have counseled the soldiers to abandon the military.

ii. Pacifist Response: It is an Argument Drawn from Silence

Like the pacifist response to the fact that Jesus does not rebuke Peter for carrying a sword (*machaira*), pacifists argue that the argument that John the Baptist, Jesus and Peter never command the Romans soldiers that they encounter to abandon the military is in fact an endorsement of the military is an argument drawn from silence. Because John the Baptist, Jesus and Paul never endorse military service explicitly, we should not assume that they supported it. Pacifists respond to the passages cited by just war theorists as follows:

- In John the Baptist's encounter with Roman soldiers, he forbids them from violently oppressing anyone (Luke 3:14). His recommendation is not intended as an exhaustive list for achieving perfection, but rather, as a recommendation for entering the Kingdom of God.
- Jesus praises a Roman centurion for his faith (Mat 8). Jesus' praise was directed at the centurion's faith, not his profession; the centurion was able to trust in Jesus to the point that he did not need to see the healing in person. This willingness to believe Jesus despite a natural inclination to "see it to believe it" is the subject of Jesus' praise. Jesus is looking for people who are willing to trust him even when they do not understand God's reasoning or even agree with his reasoning;
- God uses a Roman centurion to teach Peter that the new covenant is intended for the Gentiles as well as for the Jews (Acts 10); the book of Acts also references a "devout soldier" (Acts 10). These stories simply demonstrates that God can use anyone, in any profession, to further his purposes and that there can be devout members of any profession. The passages do not necessarily endorse the military profession.

b. Verses that Endorse Pacifism

a. *Sermon on the Mount: "Do Not Resist an Evil Person"; "Turn the Other Cheek"; "Love Your Enemy" and "Pray for Those Who Persecute You" (Mat 5:38-44)*

i. The Beatitudes

> Mat 5:1 And seeing the multitudes, He went up on a mountain, and when He was seated His disciples came to Him.
> Mat 5:2 Then He opened His mouth and taught them, saying:
>
> Mat 5:3 "Blessed are the poor in spirit, For theirs is the kingdom of heaven.

Mat 5:4   Blessed are those who mourn, For they shall be comforted.

Mat 5:5 Blessed are the meek, For they shall inherit the earth.

Mat 5:6   Blessed are those who hunger and thirst for righteousness, For they shall be filled.

Mat 5:7 Blessed are the merciful, For they shall obtain mercy.

Mat 5:8 Blessed are the pure in heart, For they shall see God.

Mat 5:9 Blessed are the peacemakers, For they shall be called sons of God.

Mat 5:10   Blessed are those who are persecuted for righteousness' sake, For theirs is the kingdom of heaven.

Mat 5:11 "Blessed are you when they revile and persecute you, and say all kinds of evil against you falsely for My sake.

Mat 5:12 Rejoice and be exceedingly glad, for great is your reward in heaven, for so they persecuted the prophets who were before you.

ii. Salt and Light

Mat 5:13 "You are the salt of the earth; but if the salt loses its flavor, how shall it be seasoned? It is then good for nothing but to be thrown out and trampled underfoot by men.

Mat 5:14 "You are the light of the world. A city that is set on a hill cannot be hidden.

Mat 5:15 Nor do they light a lamp and put it under a basket, but on a lampstand, and it gives light to all who are in the house.

Mat 5:16 Let your light so shine before men, that they may see your good works and glorify your Father in heaven.

iii. Fulfillment of the Law

Mat 5:17 "Do not think that I came to destroy the Law or the Prophets. I did not come to destroy but to fulfill.

Mat 5:18 For assuredly, I say to you, till heaven and earth pass away, one jot or one tittle will by no means pass from the law till all is fulfilled.

Mat 5:19 Whoever therefore breaks one of the least of these commandments, and teaches men so, shall be called least in the kingdom of heaven; but whoever does and teaches them, he shall be called great in the kingdom of heaven.

Mat 5:20 For I say to you, that unless your righteousness exceeds the righteousness of the scribes and Pharisees, you will by no means enter the kingdom of heaven.

iv. Heightening of Mosaic Legal Standards to Moral Standards: The Six Antithesis

(1) First Antithesis: Murder (Mat 5:21-25)

> Mat 5:21 "You have heard that it was said to those of old, 'YOU SHALL NOT MURDER, and whoever murders will be in danger of the judgment.'
> Mat 5:22 But I say to you that whoever is angry with his brother without a cause shall be in danger of the judgment. And whoever says to his brother, 'Raca!' shall be in danger of the council. But whoever says, 'You fool!' shall be in danger of hell fire.
> Mat 5:23 Therefore if you bring your gift to the altar, and there remember that your brother has something against you,
> Mat 5:24 leave your gift there before the altar, and go your way. First be reconciled to your brother, and then come and offer your gift.
> Mat 5:25 Agree with your adversary quickly, while you are on the way with him, lest your adversary deliver you to the judge, the judge hand you over to the officer, and you be thrown into prison.

(2) Second Antithesis: Adultery (Mat 5:27-30)

> Mat 5:27 "You have heard that it was said to those of old, 'YOU SHALL NOT COMMIT ADULTERY.'
> Mat 5:28 But I say to you that whoever looks at a woman to lust for her has already committed adultery with her in his heart.
> Mat 5:29 If your right eye causes you to sin, pluck it out and cast it from you; for it is more profitable for you that one of your members perish, than for your whole body to be cast into hell.
> Mat 5:30 And if your right hand causes you to sin, cut it off and cast it from you; for it is more profitable for you that one of your members perish, than for your whole body to be cast into hell.

(3) Third Antithesis: Divorce (Mat 5:31-32)

> Mat 5:31 "Furthermore it has been said, 'Whoever divorces his wife, let him give her a certificate of divorce.'
> Mat 5:32 But I say to you that whoever divorces his wife for any reason except sexual immorality causes her to commit adultery; and whoever marries a woman who is divorced commits adultery.

(4) Fourth Antithesis: Oaths (Mat 5:33-37)

> Mat 5:33 "Again you have heard that it was said to those of old, 'You shall not swear falsely, but shall perform your oaths to the Lord.'
> Mat 5:34 But I say to you, do not swear at all: neither by heaven, for it is God's throne;
> Mat 5:35 nor by the earth, for it is His footstool; nor by Jerusalem, for it is the city of the great King.
> Mat 5:36 Nor shall you swear by your head, because you cannot make one hair white or black.
> Mat 5:37 But let your 'Yes' be 'Yes,' and your 'No,' 'No.' For whatever is more than these is from the evil one.

(5) Fifth Antithesis: Do Not Resist an Evil Person; Abolishing *Lex Talionis*; Turn the Other Cheek (Mat 5:38-42)

(a) Overview

In the first four and the sixth antithesis, Jesus heightens the Mosaic legal standards. In the fifth antithesis, however, Jesus overrules the Mosaic law.

> Mat 5:38 "You have heard that it was said, 'AN EYE FOR AN EYE AND A TOOTH FOR A TOOTH.'
> Mat 5:39 But I tell you *not to resist an evil person*. But *whoever slaps you on your right cheek, turn the other to him also*.
> Mat 5:40 If anyone wants to sue you and take away your tunic, let him have your cloak also.
> Mat 5:41 And whoever compels you to go one mile, go with him two.
> Mat 5:42 Give to him who asks you, and from him who wants to borrow from you do not turn away.

Here, Jesus overrules the principle of *lex talionis*, which was established in the Mosaic law ("if any harm follows, then you shall give life for life, eye for eye, tooth for tooth, hand for hand, foot for foot, burn for burn, wound for wound, stripe for stripe" (Exo 21:23-25)) and reiterated in the Psalms ("O daughter of Babylon, who are to be destroyed, Happy the one who repays you as you have served us!" (Psa 137:8)).

Consider also Richard B Hays' commentary:

> The *lex talionis* ("An eye for an eye and a tooth for a tooth") may have originated, as most commentators note, as a rule limiting the vengeance that might be exacted by an aggrieved party: that is, no more than an eye for an eye. That is how the rule apparently functions in Exodus 21:24. If the saying is understood in those terms, then Matthew 5:39 can be understood as conforming to the pattern of heightening the Torah's demand: where the Torah restricts retaliation, Jesus forbids it altogether.
> In Deuteronomy 19:15-21, however, the *lex talionis* has a prescriptive function. False witnesses are to be punished with exactly the same punishment that would have been inflicted on the one whom they have falsely accused. Deuteronomy insists that the punishment must be exacted as a deterrent to future offenses" (Richard B. Hays, The Moral Vision of the New Testament, pp. 324-25).

The text of Deuteronomy 19:18-19 states: "And the judges shall make careful inquiry, and indeed, if the witness is a false witness, who has testified falsely against his brother, then you shall do to him as he thought to have done to his brother; so you shall put away the evil from among you." Thus, in commanding His followers not to exact vengeance, Jesus overrules the text of Deuteronomy 19:18-19, which directly commands that the Judges do to a false witness that which he sought to do to his brother.

(b) Just War Theorists' Answer

As discussed above, pacifists view Matthew 5:38-42 as overruling Old Testament *lex talionis* and replacing it with a new law of forbearing mercy that does not express resent or retaliation but rather willingly accepts retaliation. Some just war theorists argue that Matthew 5:38-42 is not intended by Jesus to overrule Old Testament *lex talionis*, but rather, to provide narrow exceptions to its general application.

Jesus begins the fifth antithesis with the words "You have heard that it was said, 'an eye for an eye and a tooth for a tooth'" (Mat 5:38). Here, he articulates a principle based in Exodus and Deuteronomy that either limits the amount of retaliation that is permitted or commands that retaliation equal to the original offense be enacted. However, in the verses following Matthew 5:38, Jesus is not abolishing *lex talionis*, but rather, He is providing three very specific exceptions to its general application:

- "[W]hoever slaps you on your right cheek, turn the other to him also" (Mat 5:39);
- "If anyone wants to sue you and take away your tunic, let him have your cloak also" (Mat 5:40);
- "[W]hoever compels you to go one mile, go with him two" (Mat 5:41).

In all other cases, Christians are to enact against wrongdoers the same wrong that the wrongdoers committed—an eye for an eye and a tooth for a tooth.

(c) Pacifists' Reply

While the just war theorist's interpretation of Matthew 5:38-42 correctly points out that Jesus never intended to abolish the Old Testament law, including *lex talionis*, it fails to recognize that Jesus fulfilled it. Jesus says the same just before he pronounces the six antitheses in the sermon on the mount: "Do not think that I came to destroy the Law or the Prophets. I did not come to destroy but to fulfill" (Mat 5:17).

To interpret *lex talionis* as a law of continuous application would be a contradiction of Christ's fulfillment of the Old Testament law when He died on the cross. Moreover, to hold that the principle of "an eye for an eye" and "a tooth for a tooth" in

Exodus 21:24 and Deuteronomy 19:15-21 continues to apply to Christians today would by corollary mean that the rest of the Old Testament law also applies to Christians; there is no reasonable basis to state that *lex talionis* applies but other laws, such as, for example, the application of the death penalty to anyone who profanes the Sabbath (Exo 31:14) or curses his parents (Exo 21:17), would not also apply.

To adopt such a view, however, would be a flagrant contradiction of the conclusions drawn at the Council of Jerusalem (Acts 15), which the Apostles convened when certain men taught that without circumcision under the rule of Moses, there is no salvation (Acts 15:1). When the Apostles and the rulers of the church convened and weighed the question (Acts 15:6), Peter got up and addressed the group, saying "Why then are you testing God, by putting on their necks a yoke so hard that not even our fathers or we were strong enough for it?" (Acts 15:10). James then said (Acts 15:13) that his decision was to not put trouble in the way of those who from among the Gentiles are turned to God (Acts 15:19) but that they only be ordered to keep themselves from things offered to false gods, from the evil desires of the body, from the flesh of animals put to death in ways against the law and from blood (Acts 15:20). The church then sent men from among them to Antioch with Paul and Barnabas (Acts 15:22) with a letter saying that Christians were only required to keep from things offered to false gods, from blood, from things put to death in ways which are against the law and from the evil desires of the body (Acts 15:29). No mention of retaining *lex talionis* was made by the Council.

As such, it is to be understood by Christians that *lex talionis*, like the rest of the corpus of the Old Testament law, was fulfilled by Christ, and Christians are now subject to a heightened standard of morality, one that does not enact evil for evil, but bears abuse with patience and restraint.

(6) Sixth Antithesis: Love Your Enemy; Pray for Those Who Persecute You (Mat 5:43-48) (Problematic Text)

> Mat 5:43   "You have heard that it was said, 'YOU SHALL LOVE YOUR NEIGHBOR and hate your enemy.'
> Mat 5:44   But I say to you, *love your enemies*, bless those who curse you, do good to those who hate you, and *pray for those who spitefully use you and persecute you*,
> Mat 5:45   that you may be sons of your Father in heaven; for He makes His sun rise on the evil and on the good, and sends rain on the just and on the unjust.
> Mat 5:46   For if you love those who love you, what reward have you? Do not even the tax collectors do the same?
> Mat 5:47   And if you greet your brethren only, what do you do more than others? Do not even the tax collectors do so?
> Mat 5:48   Therefore you shall be perfect, just as your Father in heaven is perfect.

b. *God Allows Evil to Fall Upon the Just and the Unjust (Mat 5:45)*

Just after His teaching to "love your enemy" and "pray for those who persecute you" (Mat 5:44), Jesus teaches that God:

> Mat 5:45   makes His sun rise on the evil and on the good, and sends rain on the just and on the unjust.

God allows bad things to happen even to the just and upright. God thus has control over what happens to us, and yet he still allows bad to happen because he wants His followers to exercise the values of the Kingdom of Heaven, so that when threatened with physical violence, the values of Heaven are demonstrated and God is glorified when His followers refuse to give in to fear and instead choose to show faith and love in the face of violence and death.

c. *"Harmless As Doves" (Mat 10:16); "Do not Fear Those Who Kill the Body" (Mat 10:28); "Whoever Desires to Save His Life Will Lose It" (Mat 16:25)*

i.   Be "Harmless As Doves" (Mat 10:16)

Jesus commanded his disciples to "be wise as serpents and harmless as doves" (Mat 10:16). One cannot reconcile taking up arms with being as "harmless as doves." In his commentary, Barnes interprets this as a command "not to provoke danger, not to do injury, and thus make their fellow-men justly enraged against them."

ii. "Do not Fear Those Who Kill the Body but Cannot Kill the Soul" (Mat 10:28)

Jesus emphasizes that it is the soul, not the body, that must be of our concern. Unlike the body, the soul cannot be attacked or defended with physical weapons.

> Mat 10:28 And do not fear those who kill the body but cannot kill the soul. But rather fear Him who is able to destroy both soul and body in hell.
> Mat 10:29 Are not two sparrows sold for a copper coin? And not one of them falls to the ground apart from your Father's will.
> Mat 10:30 But the very hairs of your head are all numbered.
> Mat 10:31 Do not fear therefore; you are of more value than many sparrows.

iii. "Whoever Desires to Save His Life Will Lose It" (Mat 16:25)

Jesus emphasizes the futility of trying to save his life, for whoever tries to save his life will lose it:

> Mat 16:25 For whoever desires to save his life will lose it, but whoever loses his life for My sake will find it.

d. *"All who Take the Sword Perish by the Sword" (Mat 26:52)*

> Mat 26:51 And suddenly, one of those who were with Jesus stretched out his hand and drew his sword, struck the servant of the high priest, and cut off his ear.

Mat 26:52 Jesus said, "Put your sword in its place, for *all who take the sword will perish by the sword.*"
Mat 26:53 Or do you think that I cannot now pray to My Father, and He will provide Me with more than twelve legions of angels?
Mat 26:54 How then could the Scriptures be fulfilled, that it must happen thus?"

e. *Jesus Rebukes the Disciples for Suggesting Punishing the Samaritans for Not Receiving Him (Luke 9:51)*

i. Text

Luke 9:51 Now it came to pass, when the time had come for Him to be received up, that He steadfastly set His face to go to Jerusalem,
Luke 9:52 and sent messengers before His face. And as they went, they entered a village of the Samaritans, to prepare for Him.
Luke 9:53 But they did not receive Him, because His face was set for the journey to Jerusalem.
Luke 9:54 And when His disciples James and John saw this, they said, "Lord, do You want us to command fire to come down from heaven and consume them, just as Elijah did?"
Luke 9:55 But He turned and rebuked them, and said, "You do not know what manner of spirit you are of.
Luke 9:56 For the Son of Man did not come to destroy men's lives but to save them." And they went to another village.

ii. Analysis

Barnes commentary states that Jesus' words in Luke 9:55 ("You do not know what manner of spirit you are of") indicates that the disciples, though appearing to be motivated by a love for Christ and desire to honor Him, were actually motivated by a vengeful spite towards the Samaritans. Barnes writes:

Ye know not what manner of spirit ye are of - You suppose that you are actuated by a proper love for me; but you know not yourselves. It is rather a love of revenge; rather revengeful feelings toward the "Samaritans" than proper feelings toward "me." We learn here:

1. That "apparent" zeal for God may be only improper opposition toward our fellow-men.

2. That people, when they wish to honor God, should examine their spirit, and see if there is not lying at the bottom of their professed zeal for God some bad feeling toward their fellow-men.

3. That the highest opposition which Jesus met with was not inconsistent with "his" loving those who opposed him, and with his seeking to do them good.

Clarke's analysis largely reiterates these points. He writes that in Luke 9:55, Jesus meant:

> And ye do not consider that the zeal which you feel springs from an evil principle, being more concerned for your own honor than for the honor of God. The disciples of that Christ who died for his enemies should never think of avenging themselves on their persecutors.

In seeking to destroy one's enemy, a person professing Christ may be more concerned with (or as concerned with) revenge and hatred than in honoring God. Christ thus forbids us from enacting revenge at all.

f. The Example of Jesus' Disciple Stephen (Acts 7:60)

Those who argue that Christ's self-sacrificial example was not normative for Christians, but was merely an act required for the Scriptures to be fulfilled (Mat 26:54), need look no further than the lives of the early martyrs to find the flaw in their reasoning. We can consider the account of the disciple Stephen, who like Jesus willingly underwent death at the hands of his persecutors and false accusers, never lifting a finger in his defense, but rather, kneeling down and crying before those who had dragged him away to stone him, "Lord, do not charge them with this sin" (Acts 7:60).

g. Paul's Letters: "Live Peaceably with All Men" (Rom 12:18); "Though We Walk in the Flesh, We do Not War According to

the Flesh" (2Co 10:3); "We do Not Wrestle against Flesh and Blood, but against Principalities and Powers" (Eph 6:12)

i.   Verses

Rom 12:18 If it is possible, as much as depends on you, live peaceably with all men.

2Co 10:3   For though we walk in the flesh, we do not war according to the flesh.
2Co 10:4   For the weapons of our warfare are not carnal but mighty in God for pulling down strongholds,
2Co 10:5   casting down arguments and every high thing that exalts itself against the knowledge of God, bringing every thought into captivity to the obedience of Christ,

Eph 6:11 Put on the whole armor of God, that you may be able to stand against the wiles of the devil.
Eph 6:12 For we do not wrestle against flesh and blood, but against principalities, against powers, against the rulers of the darkness of this age, against spiritual hosts of wickedness in the heavenly places.
Eph 6:13 Therefore take up the whole armor of God, that you may be able to withstand in the evil day, and having done all, to stand.
Eph 6:14 Stand therefore, having girded your waist with truth, having put on the breastplate of righteousness,
Eph 6:15 and having shod your feet with the preparation of the gospel of peace;
Eph 6:16 above all, taking the shield of faith with which you will be able to quench all the fiery darts of the wicked one.
Eph 6:17 And take the helmet of salvation, and the sword of the Spirit, which is the word of God;
Eph 6:18 praying always with all prayer and supplication in the Spirit, being watchful to this end with all perseverance and supplication for all the saints--

ii. Analysis

Although we walk in the flesh, our war is not according to the flesh (2Co 10:3). It is not a battle in the physical, but in the spiritual realm. We wage this battle not through arms destroyed to kill the body, but through spiritual weapons: "the whole armor of God" (Eph 6:13); "truth" and "the breastplate of righteousness" (Eph 6:14); "the gospel of peace" (Eph 6:15); "the shield of faith" (Eph 6:16); "the helmet of salvation and the sword of the Spirit" (Eph 6:17).

h.   Revelation: "He Who Kills with the Sword Must Be Killed with the Sword" (Rev 13:10)

The Revelation of Jesus Christ declares: " He who leads into captivity shall go into captivity; he who kills with the sword must be killed with the sword. Here is the patience and the faith of the saints" (Rev 13:10).

CHAPTER 5. CHRISTIANS ARE TO FORGIVE; GOD USES GOVERNMENT TO ENACT VENGEANCE

A. NORMS FOR INDIVIDUAL CHRISTIANS

Paul taught that Christians are not to not repay "evil for evil" (Rom 12:17) or exact vengeance (Rom 12:19). We are instead to "live peaceably with all men" (Rom 12:17) and "overcome evil with good" (Rom 12:21):

> Rom 12:17 Repay no one *evil for evil*. Have regard for good things in the sight of all men.
> Rom 12:18 If it is possible, as much as depends on you, *live peaceably with all men*.
> Rom 12:19 Beloved, *do not avenge yourselves*, but rather give place to wrath; for it is written, "vengeance is mine, i will repay," says the Lord.
> Rom 12:20 Therefore "if your enemy is hungry, feed him; if he is thirsty, give him a drink; for in so doing you will heap coals of fire on his head."
> Rom 12:21 Do not be overcome by evil, but *overcome evil with good*.

B. NORMS FOR THE GOVERNMENT

The government, in contrast, follows an entirely different framework. The authority is "God's minister" and "an avenger to execute wrath on him who practices evil" (Rom 13:4).

> Rom 13:1 Let every soul be subject to the governing authorities. For there is no authority except from God, and the authorities that exist are *appointed by God*.
> Rom 13:2 Therefore whoever resists the authority resists the ordinance of God, and those who resist will bring judgment on themselves.
> Rom 13:3 For rulers are not a terror to good works, but to evil. Do you want to be unafraid of the authority? Do what is good, and you will have praise from the same.
> Rom 13:4 For he is *God's minister* to you for good. But if you do evil, be afraid; for he does not bear the sword in vain; for he is God's minister, *an avenger to execute wrath on him who practices evil*.
> Rom 13:5 Therefore you must be subject, not only because of wrath but also for conscience' sake.

The authority is "appointed" by God (Rom 13:1) for this purpose. We are therefore to "be subject" (Rom 13:5), support the authorities by paying taxes (Rom 13:6-7) and pray for them (1Ti 2:1-2).

> Rom 13:6 For because of this you also pay taxes, for they are God's ministers attending continually to this very thing.
> Rom 13:7 Render therefore to all their due: taxes to whom taxes are due, customs to whom customs, fear to whom fear, honor to whom honor.

> 1Ti 2:1 Therefore I exhort first of all that supplications, prayers, intercessions, and giving of thanks be made for all men,
> 1Ti 2:2 for kings and all who are in authority, that we may lead a quiet and peaceable life in all godliness and reverence.

C. CONCLUSION

Thus, individual Christians are to refrain from avenging wrongdoers or using violence; God has instituted civil authorities to undertake these functions.

APPENDICES

DWIGHT D. EISENHOWER'S WORDS ON WAR

"Every gun that is made, every warship launched, every rocket fired signifies, in the final sense, a theft from those who hunger and are not fed, those who are cold and are not clothed.

"This world in arms is not spending money alone. It is spending the sweat of its laborers, the genius of its scientists, the hopes of its children.

"The cost of one modern heavy bomber is this: a modern brick school in more than 30 cities. It is two electric power plants, each serving a town of 60,000 population. It is two fine, fully equipped hospitals. It is some fifty miles of concrete pavement. We pay for a single fighter plane with a half million bushels of wheat.

"We pay for a single destroyer with new homes that could have housed more than 8,000 people. This is, I repeat, the best way of life to be found on the road the world has been taking.

"This is not a way of life at all, in any true sense. Under the cloud of threatening war, it is humanity hanging from a cross of iron. ...

"Is there no other way the world may live?

"When people speak to you about a preventive war, you tell them to go and fight it. I hate war as only a soldier who has lived it can, only as one who has seen its brutality, its futility, its stupidity. After my experience, I have come to hate war. War settles nothing."

- Dwight D. Eisenhower

"GOTT MIT UNS"

A slogan of the German Christian political organization Deutsche Christen, "Gott Mit Uns," means "God With Us."

The propaganda of the German government, coupled with the unthinking submission of the German people who believed the lies they were told, Germany was led into war and caused the most effusion of blood and destruction the known in modern history. The German people were mistakenly led to believe that God would lead and bless their nation and their efforts, which was clearly not the case.

BIBLIOGRAPHY

Corey, David D., *The Just War Tradition: An Introduction* (American Ideals and Institutions) (Intercollegiate Studies Institute, 2012)

Cowles, C.S., Merrill, Eugene H., Gard, Daniel L., Longman, Trempler III, Gundry, Standley N. (Series Editor), *Show them No Mercy: 4 Views on God and Canaanite Genocide* (Zondervan, 2003).

Craigie, Peter C., *The Problem of War in the Old Testament* (Grand Rapids: Eerdmans, 1978).

Jenkins, Philip, *Laying Down the Sword: Why We Can't Ignore the Bible's Violent Verses* (HarperOne, 2012)

Mattox, John Mark, *St. Augustine and the Theory of Just War* (Bloomsbury Studies in Philosophy) (Bloomsbury Academic, 2009)

Made in the USA
Las Vegas, NV
12 January 2022

41194014R00039